THE TOWN OF NO
&
MY BROTHER RUNNING

THE TOWN OF NO
&
MY BROTHER
RUNNING

POEMS BY

Wesley McNair

DAVID R. GODINE, *Publisher*

BOSTON

1997 by
blisher, Inc.

etts 01773

The Town of No and *My Brother Running* were
originally published as two separate volumes by
David R. Godine, Boston, in 1989 and 1993.

Library of Congress Cataloging-in-Publication Data
McNair, Wesley.
[Town of No]
The Town of No ; & My brother running : poems /
by Wesley McNair. — 1st ed.
p.   cm.
I. McNair, Wesley. My brother running.
II. Title. III. Title: My brother running.
ps3563.c388a6   1996
811'.54—dc20   95-35338 cip

ISBN: 1-56792-056-x

First printing, 1997
This book was printed on acid-free paper
Manufactured in Canada

Contents

THE TOWN OF NO

I. MUTE

II. THE BEFORE PEOPLE

III. GHOSTS

IV. THE ABANDONMENT

V. THE REVIVAL

MY BROTHER RUNNING

Part One

WALKING IN DARK TOWN

Part Two

MY BROTHER RUNNING · 121

THE TOWN OF NO

for Diane

MUTE

THE LAST TIME SHORTY TOWERS FETCHED THE COWS

In the only story we have
of Shorty Towers, it is five o'clock
and he is dead drunk on his roof
deciding to fetch the cows. How
he got in this condition, shingling
all afternoon, is what the son-in-law,
the one who made the back pasture
into a golf course, can't figure out. So,
with an expression somewhere between shock
and recognition, he just watches Shorty
pull himself up to his not-so-
full height, square his shoulders,
and sigh that small sigh as if caught
once again in an invisible swarm
of bees. Let us imagine, in that moment
just before he turns to the roof's edge
and the abrupt end of the joke
which is all anyone thought to remember
of his life, Shorty is listening
to what seems to be the voice
of a lost heifer, just breaking
upward. And let us think that when he walks
with such odd purpose down that hill
jagged with shingles, he suddenly feels it
open into the wide, incredibly green
meadow where all the cows are.

REMEMBERING APRONS

Who recalls the darkness
of your other life,
sewn shut

around feed grain,
or remembers your release
to join your sisters,

the dishcloths, now
ampleness and holes?
Not the absent hands

which tied you
behind the back,
already forgetting.

How thoughtlessly
they used you,
old stove-gloves,

soft baskets
for tomatoes, and yet
how wonderfully

such being
left out
shows your inclusion!

Oh tough dresses
without closets,
lovely petticoats that flashed

beneath the frayed
hemlines of barncoats
all over Vermont.

❦ THE HAND

Her small life as a daughter
and sister and aunt

was a story of hands, the one
which they knew her by,

high up at her side
like a fin,

the other which looked like theirs,
so nobody saw it

find by itself the strings
of her apron,

or lift eggs out of a nest
between fingers,

or loosen and close
the west window

in dusk, its palm pressed
to the vanishing glass.

THE SHOOTING

There are no photographs
of the two farmhands,
each born on the other's
birthday, with the same face.

There is no story
of why whatever
it was held them together,
closer than brothers,

broke on that day.
Only the memory
of him, the quiet one,
whispering the words

of the other
before they were said.
Only that after they
found him, holding the face

that looked like his,
and called his name
over and over, they never
mistook which one he was.

KILLING THE ANIMALS

The chickens cannot
find their heads
though they search for them,
falling in the grass.

And the great bulls
remain on their knees,
unable to remember
how to stand.

The goats cannot find their voices.
They run quickly
on their sides,
watching the sky.

THE NAME

At the end of her life,
when the fire
lifted her house away,
and her left side
vanished in a stroke,
and she woke
in that white room
without apron or shoes,
she searched each face
until she found her twice-
divorced daughter, the one
she'd always said wasn't
over Fool's Hill yet,
and, taking her hand
as if they'd all along
been close, began
to call the name
the frightened daughter
never heard before,
not father or brother.

🌿 MINA BELL'S COWS

O where are Mina Bell's cows who gave no milk
and grazed on her dead husband's farm?
Each day she walked with them into the field,
loving their swayback dreaminess more
than the quickness of any dog or chicken.
Each night she brought them grain in the dim barn,
holding their breath in her hands.
O when the lightning struck Daisy and Bets,
her son dug such great holes in the yard
she could not bear to watch him.
And when the baby, April, growing old
and wayward, fell down the hay chute,
Mina just sat in the kitchen, crying, "Ape,
Ape," as if she called all three cows,
her walleyed girls who never would come home.

MUTE

Once, on the last ice-hauling,
the sled went through the surface
of the frozen pond,
pulling the son under
the thrashing hooves
of horses. Listening for him

after all her tears was perhaps
what drew the mother
into that silence. Long afternoons
she sat with the daughter,
speaking in the sign language
they invented together,
going deaf to the world.

How, exactly, did they touch
their mouths? What was the thought
of the old man on the porch
growing so drunk by nightfall
he could not hear
mosquitoes in his ears?

There is so much no one remembers
about the farm where sound,
even the bawling of the unmilked cows,
came to a stop. Even the man's name,

which neighbors must have spoken
passing by in twilight, on their way
to forgetting it forever.

THE BEFORE PEOPLE

WHERE ARE THE QUELCHES?

O what has happened to Quelch?
Where is his great belly

and cigarette-pack breast, and where
is the thin wife who burped

spaghetti each night out
of the can, and gave such parties

the women shrieked through the wall,
the men rained urine over

and over, and the fist
of the gramophone fell asleep

unwinding the lovesick voice
of Gene Autry. Where are the Quelches

and what do they have to do
with this shy, stooped man

shaking my hand and this woman,
so precisely speaking their names?

THE BEFORE PEOPLE

There is a moment when they turn
to the ads that are meant for them
and are happy, a moment when the fat woman
thinks of melting her body away in seven days,
and the shut-in imagines big money
without leaving his home. Slowly,
as if for the first time, they read
the italics of their deepest wishes:
Made $5,000 in first month,
Used to call me Fatty, and all
the people with no confidence,
no breasts, or hair in the wrong places
find pictures of the amazing results
in their own states. They have overlooked
the new techniques, and the research
of doctors in Germany, they know that now,
suddenly so pleased they can hardly
remember being sad in this, their moment,
before, just before they lie back on the beds
in their small rooms and think about how foolish
they are or how farfetched it is or anything
except the actual photographs of their dreams.

BIG CARS

Ten years later
they arrive on the thruway,
pulling winged fenders and smiling
a lane wide—big cars,
old floats that took a wrong
corner somewhere and lost
the American dream parade. Around them

the strange, grilleless
cars of the future
hum at their tires—tiny aliens
of a planet out of gas.

To think of their long trip
just beginning—the irrepressible fuel
rising everywhere into their tanks!
For the first time, armrests
unfolded out of seats;
out of the armrests, ashtrays!
Maps fell open to the new roads

which led them, finally, here
to the right lanes of America—
the antiques of optimism
nobody understands or wants
except the poor. Or dictators

driving down boulevards in some country
where the poor do not have cars
and run alongside until it seems
that they themselves are riding
on soft shocks, under a sun roof,
toward the great plenty of the New World.

BEGGARS

the one without legs reaches
up as if he would have us pull him
out of the sidewalk

we cannot pull him
our money will not help
the big-chested man whose legs
are folded in front of him
like socks

when we turn an old man
is making an earnest expression
with half of his face
two sisters remember songs
behind their white eyes

where do beggars go when the streets
are full of rain
the man in a cart rowing

his half-body away
with his hands

the girl on wood crutches
doing her slow breaststroke
into our dreams

THE BALD SPOT

It nods
behind me
as I speak
at the meeting.

All night
while I sleep
it stares
into the dark.

The bald spot
is bored.
Tired of waiting
in the office,

sick of following me
into sex.
It traces
and retraces

itself,
dreaming
the shape
of worlds

beyond its world.
Far away
it hears the laughter
of my colleagues,

the swift sure
sound of my voice.
The bald spot
says nothing.

It peers
out from hair
like the face
of a doomed man

going blanker
and blanker,
walking backwards
into my life.

HAIR ON TELEVISION

On the soap opera the doctor
explains to the young woman with cancer
that each day is beautiful.

Hair lifts from their heads
like clouds, like something to eat.

It is the hair of the married couple
getting in touch with their real feelings for the first
time on the talk show,

the hair of young people on the beach
drinking Cokes and falling in love.

And the man who took the laxative and waters his garden
next day with the hose wears the hair

so dark and wavy even his grandchildren are amazed,
and the woman who never dreamed tampons
could be so convenient wears it.

For the hair is changing people's lives.
It is growing like wheat above the faces

of game show contestants opening the doors
of new convertibles, of prominent businessmen opening
their hearts to Christ, and it is growing

straight back from the foreheads of vitamin experts,
detergent and dog food experts
helping ordinary housewives discover

how to be healthier, get clothes cleaner
and serve dogs meals they love in the hair.

And over and over on television the housewives,
and the news teams bringing all the news faster
and faster, and the new breed of cops winning the fight

against crime are smiling, pleased to be at their best
proud to be among the literally millions of Americans

everywhere who have tried the hair, compared the hair
and will never go back to life before the active,
the caring, the successful, the incredible hair.

At first the job is a cinch like
they said. They manage to get the bank teller
a couple of times in the head
and blow the vault door so high
it never comes down. Money bags line the shelves
inside like groceries. They are rich, richer
than they can believe. Above his purple suit the boss
is grinning half outside of his face.
Two goons are taking the dough in their arms
like their first women. For a minute nobody sees
the little thug with the beanie is sweating drops
the size of hot dogs and pointing
straight up. There is a blue man flying
down through the skylight and landing with his arms
crossed. They exhale their astonishment
into small balloons. "What the," they say,
"What the," watching their bullets drop
off his chest over and over. Soon he begins to talk
about the fight against evil, beating them half to death
with his fists. Soon they are picking themselves up
from the floor of the prison. Out the window Superman
is just clearing a tall building and couldn't care less
when they shout his name through the bars.
"We're trapped! We got no chance!"
they say, tightening their teeth,

thinking, like you, how it always gets down
to the same old shit: no fun, no dough,
no power to rise out of their bodies.

⚜ THE FAT ENTER HEAVEN

It is understood, with the clarity possible only
in heaven, that none have loved food
better than these. Angels gather to admire
their small mouths and their arms, round
as the fenders of Hudson Hornets. In their past
they have been among the world's most meek,
the farm boy who lived with his mother,
the grade-school teacher who led the flag salute
with expression, day after day. Now
their commonplace lives, the guilt
about weight, the ridicule fade and disappear.
They come to the table arrayed with perfect food
shedding their belts and girdles for the last time.
Here, where fat itself is heavenly,
they fill their plates and float upon the sky.

THE FAT PEOPLE
OF THE OLD DAYS

Oddly, being so large
gave them a sense
of possibility.

Women with huge upper arms
felt freer.

Children never stopped opening
the landscapes of flesh
which grew in their hands.

The few thin ones
were called "chinless"
because their chins seemed
indistinguishable from their necks.

No one knows when the thin ones
began to seem beautiful,
when the fat people first worried
about weight.

A woman came to fear
her elbows and knees
were sinking into dimples.

A man believed his chin,
which shook when he talked,
was also speaking.

For many years the fat life continued.

Each day inside strange
houses with wide doors,
fathers rose folding themselves
into their pants.

Each night the families
dreamed of bones
hung forever in fat's
locked closet.

GHOSTS

THE THIN MAN

Once in a mirror
as it folded hair
back from its face

he discovered his eyes
earnest, lonely.
This was the beginning

of his life
inside the body,
of standing deep in the legs

of it,
held
in its elbowless arms.

And when it walked
he walked,
and when it slept

he dreamed of drowning
under its lakes
of skin.

Oh the thin man
trying to get out
learned of its great

locked breasts,
its seamless chin,
the dead ends

of its hands.
And oh the heavy body
took him

to tables
of food,
and took him down

into the groaning
carnal bed.
The pitiless body took him

to a mirror
which showed
the eyes

in a face
immense and dying,
who he was.

THE LONGING OF THE FEET

At first the crawling
child makes his whole body
a foot.

One day, dazed
as if by memory,
he pulls himself up,

discovering, suddenly,
that the feet
are for carrying

hands. He is so
happy he cannot stop
taking the hands

from room to room,
learning the names
of everything he wants.

This lasts for many years
until the feet,
no longer fast enough,

lie forgotten, say,
in the office
under a desk. Above them

the rest of the body,
where the child
has come to live,

is sending its voice
hundreds of miles
through a machine.

Left to themselves
over and over,
the feet sleep,

awakening
one day
beyond the dead

conversation of the mind
and the hands.
Mute in their shoes,

your shoes
and mine,
they wait,

longing only to stand
the body
and take it

into its low,
mysterious flight
along the earth.

THE FAITH HEALER

When I turned,
it was like the father
had been walking right
toward me forever
with his eyes shut
pushing that boy,
all washed up and
dressed up and riding
above those long spokes
shooting light like
he was something more than arms
and a chest. Already
the mother was saying please,
oh please, partly to me,
partly because she heard
the sound, so soft
and far off at first
you might have never guessed it
was going to be the father
with his eyes shut, screaming.
But I knew, and I knew
even before it stopped
and he began to point
down at his son's
steel feet and whatever
was inside the dead
balloons of his pants,
the father did it. So when
he said he did it,

I was thinking of how
only his mouth was moving
in his shut face like
he had gone somewhere
outside of his body
which he could not stand.
And when he said
he did it because his son
burned the new barn down
to the ground, then shook
and shook so you could see
he was inside his body
and could never leave,
all I could think
was how the wind was moving
the tent. Lifting it up
and up around the father
who could not see it lifting,
and the mother with the no-
color dress, and that small,
still boy, all washed up
and dressed up and
looking right at me
almost like it was OK
being a chest. Which was the moment
when my own legs went out
from under me, and I woke
with the cold steel bars
of his wheelchair fast
in my hands, and shouting
like for the first

time, heal, oh heal,
over and over to the legs
that could not walk,
and to the legs
that could, and to everyone,
everywhere, who could never
get free from such sadness.

Each morning Charley
the house painter
came to work, he left
his clenched face
holding its unlit
cigar, and his old hands
moving in their dream
of painting pastel colors
on new houses that stood
in cow pastures. He
was selling sewing machines
in Brazil, just as if
thirty-five years
had never happened. This
was why each afternoon
he looked right through
the baffled landowners,
come to imagine
their twiggy sticks
would soon be trees.
Why when he got home
he never even saw
his wagging, black
habit of a farm dog,
or thought about his mother
nodding in the far room
among the water-stained
explosions of roses. Already
Charley was at his desk

down in the cellar,
waiting for his slow
legs and hands to come
and get the index cards
out from the shelves of dead
pickles and jams. Already
he was thinking
of the name for sky
with no clouds in it.
Or of the happy words
the women of Brazil said,
working the treadle.
Or of the lovely
language of the face
and legs and hands he learned
from a boy one night
beside the dark sea,
in some other life
of his lost body.

❦ BREATH

Because, remembering
how she touched
the man in the yard,
he could not look
at his wife's face,
Earl found himself alone
by the pump of the new
milking machine now out of breath,
or at a window of the barn.
Outside, where it was morning,
his father, the one-eyed man
with a cane, walked
to his old tractor
by turning himself back
to it and turning himself back
and back, as if he dragged
his body into this day
on the farm where nothing
seemed to move, even though
his father moved. And though
the cows, which had no idea
they were lifting their legs,
walked out of the barn,
and though his mother,
who had prayed this way
year after year, now stood
at the noon meal nodding
her head. Around her
the two hired men

closed their eyes,
and his father stared fast asleep
on one side of his face,
and Earl, who had never
seen them this way before,
thought of his wife
in the yard with the man
who sold him the machine.
He found again how she touched
the man's hands and chest,
and heard again as he watched
from the barn the milking machine's
great breathing. So
when he rose from the meal
with the rest, he could not go
to his home upstairs,
where she was. He walked
with his helpless father
closed away in his body,
and the hired men turning back
into the day, having no words
to say why nothing seemed
to move, though he himself
moved. And though he woke
from the thought of his wife
and the salesman and the machine's
great breath, to find himself
alone in the silo,
lifting his legs over
and over. Around him
as he packed with his feet,

the silage he had never seen
this way rained slowly
down from the far
chute, and the wood rose
so high up and windowless,
Earl felt closed away
inside the great, stopped
farm forever. And all
he could hear in his body
that walked in the silo,
then back into the day,
was his own breath,
oh, the breath,
which now vanished
in the words he spoke
to the hired men, and left
in his long whistle
which brought the cows
with no idea it had brought them,
until he found himself alone
at the pump switch, unable
to breathe. Though all
around him in the dead barn,
with its locked cows,
the milking machine began
to make its sound over
and over, which seemed
to Earl like sighing,
like his own lost breath.
He had no words to say why,
or why, when he looked

outside the barn window
and found his smiling wife
coming into the yard again,
and the salesman just
arriving in his new car, the whole
moving, breathing world seemed to him
suddenly outside. And so it was
that afternoon, he burst
open the stuck barn door
twisting its hinges,
and began to walk,
past his stooped, helpless
father, and past his mother,
who stood behind a screen window
in the house, shouting his name,
until at last he reached
the two of them, backing slowly
away as they saw the pitchfork
he held in his hands.
He had no words
to tell them how far
he had come, or how much
he desired now to join them
with his whole body,
opening his lungs as if
for the first time to take breath.

☙ THE TOWN MUSEUM

Maybe Davis lives alone
on his hill because
he found his wife
with her hand under the bib
of the hired man's bib
overalls, and maybe he speaks
to his mother in the perfectly
preserved room where she slept
and ate for twenty years,
and maybe he doesn't.
What we know is
that last spring when we looked
out of our picture windows
to find the source of all
the noise, it was Davis
at the wheel of his old
truck, too deaf to hear
he was in first gear,
and behind him a slow
semi, holding
a frail, swollen
sugarhouse like a soap bubble
on a wand. Maybe Davis is going
to try and tap the trees growing
in his fields, we said, or maybe
he is planning to take
the shrieking guinea hens
out of his trees
and put them in it;

but he wasn't.
Because the next time we looked,
the old cape from behind
the gas pumps was going right by
our pebble driveways, and then
an enormous, wasted
farmhouse, shutters
porch and all. Which was when
we called the selectman,
who just stood there
one hot day in July
watching old toothless
and shirtless Davis leading
the timbers and windows of somebody's
barn up his hill like pieces
of the last puzzle,
and who lifted
and flopped the baseball cap
back on his head and said maybe
it was some sort of
museum. What could you do
with such people, we said
across our new lawns
and kitchen bars, though
it turned out in the end he was
partly right. By this fall
when all the noise
stopped, Davis
had laid out one long
street of bent silos
and sagging sheds

and plastic-covered schoolhouse-
houses, which according to the meter-
reader, he watches from his porch
and sometimes even yells
out to. Lingering in our cars
these dark afternoons,
just back from Concord,
we think of crazy Davis
rocking and squinting
at the doors and windows
of nobody at all.
Maybe the sound
we hear, farther than wind
in our small trees,
is his voice,
high and breaking
over our roofs below.

❧ GHOSTS

When we went there,
the TV with the ghosts
would be on, and the father
talked and called out
every now and then to him,
sitting in that space
we always left around him,
Isn't it, June? or *Aren't*
you, June? And June
would laugh like only his voice
was doing it and he was somewhere
else, so when the father
turned back to us like
he was enjoying his son's
company, we could tell
he was on his way out,
too. Until at the end
he just sat saying nothing
all day into the dark.
Walking by there after chores,
we would see the blue light
from their TV, shifting
across the road in the trees,
and inside, those two dark
heads which had forgot
by this time even the cows.
So when the truck came
to take the manure-matted,
bellowing things to the slaughterhouse,

all we could say was, Thank God
for Liz. Who else
would have helped load them up,
then gone right on living
with that brother and father, dead
to the world in bib-overalls,
while all around them
the fields had begun
to forget they were fields?
Who else would have taken
that town job, punching
shoelace holes all night
into shoes? So now
when we went, there
would be Junior and his father
in the front room of the farm
they did not remember,
wearing brand-new shoes
they did not even know
they wore, watching the TV
with the ghosts. And there
would be Liz, with her apron on
over her pants, calling out
to them like they were only
deaf, *Isn't it?*
or *Aren't you?* and telling us
how at last they could have
no worries and be free.
And the thing was
that sometimes when we watched
them, watching those faces

which could no longer concentrate
on being faces, in the light
that shifted from news to ads
to sports, we could almost see
what she meant. But what
we didn't see was
that she also meant
herself. That the very
newspapers we sat on
each time we brought her milk
or eggs were Liz's own
slow way of forgetting all
her couches and chairs. Until
that last awful day
we went there,
after her father died,
and after the state car
came to take June,
and we found just flour-
bags and newspapers and Liz,
with her gray pigtail
coming undone, and no idea why
we'd left our rock-strewn fields
to come. Then all
we could think to do
was unplug that damned
TV, which by now didn't
have ghosts, only voices talking
beyond the continuous snow.
All we could do was
call her to come back

into her face and hands,
and Liz just watched
us, waving our arms,
like we weren't even there,
like we were the ghosts.

THE ABANDONMENT

TO MY FATHER,
DYING IN A SUPERMARKET

At first it is difficult
to see you
are dropping dead —

you seem lost
in thought, adjusting your tie
as if to rehearse

some imaginary speech
though of course beginning
to fall,

your mouth opening wider
than I have ever seen
a mouth,

your hands deep
in your shirt,
going down

into the cheeses, making the sound
that is not
my name,

that explains nothing
over and over,
going away

into your hands
into your face,
leaving this great body

on its knees,
the father
of my body

which holds me
in this world,
watching you go

on falling
through the Musak,
making the sound

that is not my name,
that will never
explain anything, oh father,

stranger, all dressed up
and deserting me
for the last time.

MY BROTHER INSIDE
THE REVOLVING DOORS

I see you in Chicago, twenty-five years ago,
a tall kid, surprisingly sure of yourself.
You have just arrived from the goat farm
to meet your father, the god you invented
after he left you in childhood.
It is the sunniest day you can remember,
and you walk the wide streets
of the city by his side in the dream
you have had all along of this moment,
except you are beginning to see how different
he looks, and how he does not care
about this in the same way that you do.
Which is when it happens, you are taken
inside the doors. Just like that
you are shut off from him, walking
in the weightlessness of your own fear.
And when you push your door, it leads
to other retreating doors, and again
and again, it takes you to the voice of him,
the fat man standing outside who has nothing,
suddenly, to do with your father and shouts
let go! let go! and you cannot let go.

AFTER MY STEPFATHER'S DEATH

Again it is the moment before I left home
for good, and my mother is sitting quietly
in the front seat while my stepfather pulls me
and my suitcase out of the car and begins
hurling my clothes, though now
I notice for the first time how the wind
unfolds my white shirt and puts its slow
arm in the sleeve of my blue shirt and lifts them
all into the air above our heads so beautifully
I want to shout at him to stop and look up
at what he has made, but of course when I turn
to him, a small man, bitter even this young
that the world will not go his way, my stepfather
still moves in his terrible anger, closing the trunk,
and closing himself into the car as hard as he can,
and speeding away into the last years of his life.

MY STEPFATHER'S HANDS

All day in the sun
they have dreamed
of this amber room
behind half-drawn
blinds. Tenderly,
the hand with the weak
wrist turns each leaf
of the newspaper over
to the other one
waiting to smooth it
under his eyes.
My stepfather's hands
have never been so happy.
Pieces of light stir
and float around them
in the not air, not water.

THE ABANDONMENT

Climbing on top of him and breathing
into his mouth this way she could be showing her
desire except that when she draws back
from him to make her little cries
she is turning to her young son just
coming into the room to find his father my brother
on the bed with his eyes closed and the slightest
smile on his lips as if when they
both beat on his chest as they do now
he will come back from the dream he is enjoying
so much he cannot hear her calling his name
louder and louder and the son saying get up
get up discovering both of them discovering
for the first time that all along
he has lived in this body this thing
with shut lids dangling its arms
that have nothing to do with him and everything
they can ever know the wife listening weeping
at his chest and the mute son who will never
forget how she takes the face into her hands now
as if there were nothing in the world
but the face and breathes oh
breathes into the mouth which does not breathe back.

STRING

If his last, knotted
words, this string

of thought could be undone,
if you could loosen

each frayed curse
against his life, untie

and unloop the must
and will of every

secret promise,
and ravel up page

by page the night
after night of all

he wrote, to put it safely
back into the hand

of this man everyone
now says lived

only for his family,
and built a breezeway,

deck and bar, and each
day gave everything

he had to his work,
you might never guess

these words,
this string,

how much there was
to bind him up

and hold him still.

THE REVIVAL

A TRAVELER'S ADVISORY

The main streets of towns
don't go uphill,
and the houses aren't
purple like that
tenement with one eye
clapboarded over. Never mind
how it wavers
backward, watching you
try to find second gear.
You've arrived
at the top of the town:
a closed gas station
where nobody's dog
sits, collarless,
and right next door
a church which seems
to advertise Unleaded.
Who's hung this
great front door
above no steps? No one
you'd know.
And what suspends
the avalanche
of barn? Nothing,
and you will never
escape the bump,
lifting shiny with tar.
And you won't

need the sign that says
you are leaving Don't Blink,
Can't Dance,
or Town of No.

❦ SEEING COOCH

Most winter days,
passing that
wreck of a house
all wrapped
in plastic,
you do not
find him. It just
sits by the ramp
to 89 like
a great loaf
of bread. Yet
there are times
just before
your mind closes
on the traffic
toward Concord, you see
the slow, black
coat of Cooch.
He will be out
on his failed
porch, studying
a tire or something
without a drawer.
Some nights you see him
in a room beyond
his plastic-covered
windows, moving
in the afterlife
of ruined things.

HUNT WALKING

If you could be there
with the rest, coming out

of Vernondale's store
carrying bags

in late spring, and if,
looking far down the road

where the white houses waver
in heat, you could see

for the first time
since winter, old Hunt,

the crippled man, walking
by not quite falling

down first on one side,
then on the other

holding aloft the bony
wing of his cane,

you would understand why
they have stopped

on the porch by the sign
that says Yes We Are Open,

without knowing
where they are

going, or what it is
they hold in their hands.

THE MINISTER'S DEATH

That long fall,
when the voices stopped
in the tweed mouth
of his radio, and sermons
stood behind the door
of his study in files
no one would ever again inspect,
and even the black shoes
and vestments, emptied of him,
were closed away,
they sat together Sundays
in the house, now hers —
the son wearing his suit
and water-combed hair,
and mother in a house dress,
holding the dead
man's cane. Somewhere
at the edge of the new
feeling just beginning
between them, floorlamps
bloomed triple bulbs
and windowsills sagged
with African violets,
and the old woman,
not knowing exactly how
to say his face looked lovely
in the chair, encircled
by a white aura
of doily, said nothing

at all. And the son,
not used to feeling
small inside the great
shoulderpads of his suit,
looked down at the rugs
on rugs to where the trees kept
scattering the same, soft
puzzle of sunlight
until, from time to time,
she found the words
of an old dialogue they both
could speak: "How has the weather
been this week? What time
did you start out from Keene?"

❧ THE REVIVAL

What was she to do
when the life came back
into her foot and leg,
and her arm remained a thing
that slipped down into
the wheelchair — what
but lift it out
with her well hand,
and flop it back
into her lap over
and over. Each visit
while we talked,
she carried on her wordless
conversation, patting it
and showing it how to bend
and bend, then holding it
to her breast, poor
retarded baby. Poor Mother,
prostrated in blouses
bought for the trip
she never got to take,
pulling the fingers up
from the eggless nest
of that palm, and staring
at it, just as she did
the night her arm
suddenly moved —
floated, wobbling
up into the light,

dangling the hand like
seaweed from the depths
of its strange sleep.
And then, above the shining
chrome bars of the bed,
it paused to turn
its wrist, until
we saw the miracle
was not the arm, but she
who held it there,
and spoke only to herself
in her small voice
about the mysterious power
she'd found to raise
it up, asking again
and again, "What do you
know about that?"

SUE REED WALKING

Cupboard dishes jerk past
her head,
family portraits,

colored photographs
of Keene. She is looking
straight down, amazed

by her left leg struggling
against a current
she cannot see. O

she doesn't know
when her glasses flash
up from that depth

quite where she is,
or that her sweater
twists childishly

behind her back
but never mind.
And never mind her hair

is matted
and her stiff hand
carries its useless

puff of air.
Note with what care
she places her three-

pronged cane to pull herself
back together again
and again. Listen

to her warn the cat
"I'm coming through!"
Watch Sue Reed, walking.

HAPPINESS

Why, Dot asks, stuck in the back
seat of her sister's two-door, her freckled hand
feeling the roof for the right spot
to pull her wide self up onto her left,
the unarthritic, ankle — why
does her sister, coaching outside on her cane,
have to make her laugh so, she flops
back just as she was, though now
looking wistfully out through the restaurant
reflected in her back window, she seems bigger,
and couldn't possibly mean we should go
ahead in without her, she'll be all right, and so
when you finally place the pillow behind her back
and lift her right out into the sunshine,
all four of us are happy, none more
than she, who straightens the blossoms
on her blouse, says how nice it is to get out
once in awhile, and then goes in to eat
with the greatest delicacy (oh
I could never finish all that) and aplomb
the complete roast beef dinner with apple crisp
and ice cream, just a small scoop.

THE VISIT

We were at the camp, it must have been
some afternoon that summer
when your Aunt Ruth came back
from her stroke, because her mouth
looked skeptical, almost provocative,
as if she had suddenly achieved the role
of the great lady she'd spent a lifetime
preparing for. And I remember how,
with this new dignity, she turned
to Uncle Herb's thought about the good
taste of beer on a hot day as if
he weren't wearing Bermuda shorts
and wing-tipped shoes at all,
but a loincloth. How could he
have known that she meant, if he waited
a few respectful minutes, just one
would be OK, and what was more
(the porch had got so hot, even
with the breeze), Aunt Ruth would feel
compelled to have one too? So,
what Herb came back with was beers
for everybody, even Ruth's 80-
year-old sister, do you remember,
the one who was shrinking and said Oh,
because she liked the cheese
your mother brought out or the small flowers
on the TV tray or the wind that threatened
to blow her wide hat off? It didn't,
of course, and when Ruth said No, no, no,

Herbert, we knew he could go on telling
what they did when they were younger,
because it had turned out to be
one of those wonderful days which had nothing
quite to do with wind or words. So Herb
just sat there, his white legs happy
to be free of pants, and talked — was it
about the wildest party, or how fast they drove
in his new car afterward? And while
they said they couldn't stay, they stayed
until the last light rose into the tops
of the trees around us on the lake,
and the wind suddenly stopped,
and even Aunt Ruth said how nice
it had got. Perfection
is what almost doesn't happen.

WHAT IT IS

It is not what,
carrying that
afterthought of legs,
he runs to, and not
what his interrogative, foldy
face detects
on the floor, because
it is always changing, always
turning out to be
some other bug
or bush his nose wanted,
leaving his tail
smoldering
behind, and
it is never,
after all that scratching
and lifting of leg,
enough: not even
after he joins
the dinner party, smiling
upside-down
and rolling
his testicles, not even
in his whimpering sleep,
dreaming in the tips
of his paws
that he is chasing
it, that very thing
which, scratching,

he can't quite
reach, nor sniffing find,
because in the perfect
brainlessness of dog,
he will never know
what it is.

❧ WHEN PAUL FLEW AWAY

It was the same as always,
Paul opening the big, black lung
of it with that worried look
while the cats watched
from under the stove,
but when he closed
his eyes and begun to sink
down between the straps
of his bib overalls,
it was like he died. Except
the accordion was still breathing
a waltz between his hands,
except he called back
to us every so often
from wherever he was, Shit.
Which meant everything
he had ever known
in his life up to that
moment, but this song.
Not some sock-drawer
music of getting a tune out
and then rummaging
for the chord to match,
but together, exactly like
he was breathing the thing
himself. No stomping
either, just Paul twisting
like he was after some deep
itch, only right then

he was starting to lift
out of his chair. Slowly
at first, like flypaper
in a small breeze, then
the whole enormous weight
of him hanging over the sink. God,
he was happy, and I
and the kids was laughing
and happy, when all
at once it come to me,
this is it. Paul is leaving
the old Barcolounger
stuck in second
position, and the TV on top
of the TV that don't
work, and all my hand-paintings
of strawberries as if he never
said this would be Strawberry Farm.
Hey! I said out in the yard
because he was already going
right over the roof
of the goat-shed, pumping
that song. What about you
and me? And Paul
just got farther and smaller
until he looked like a kid
unfolding paper dolls over
and over, or like
he was clapping slowly
at himself, and then
like he was opening up the wings

of some wild, black bird
he had made friends with
just before he disappeared
into the sky above the clouds
over all of Wisconsin.

THE MAN WITH THE RADIOS

Beyond the curtainless
bay windows of his room
on the side street,

he kneels
among old radios, left
from a time of belief

in radios,
some dangling fat
tails of cord

from end tables, some
in darkening corners
sprouting hairs of wire

from their great backs,
and this strange one
he has chosen,

standing on the paws
of an African cat.
The man with the radios

is so far away
in his gaze you would swear
he hears nothing,

so still you might miss
how he concentrates
on not moving

his hand. Slowly,
slowly he turns
its ridged

knob in the dark,
listening for the sound
he has prepared it for,

watching with his absent eyes
the film that clears
from a green eye.

MY BROTHER RUNNING

for my brother John

Part One

WALKING IN DARK TOWN

...
The Bravest — grope a little —
And sometimes hit a Tree
Directly on the forehead —
But as they learn to see —

Either the Darkness alters —
Or something in the sight
Adjusts itself to Midnight —
And Life steps almost straight.

Emily Dickinson, 419

WALKING IN DARK TOWN

If the houses in Dark Town turn away
carrying their yellow windows
uphill as you walk down,
nobody will care. Who's going to see
this one with the random roofline come out
to the road shrugging off the dark pines
and pausing there? Nobody's home.
And if continuing down past signs
too dark to read, you try to think why
you haven't turned back, which one
of them will help you? Not Stepless
Front Door, not Swollen Screens,
not Old Bay Windows
rolling like a damaged eye.

YOUNG MAN GOING
UPHILL WITH A BIRD

Going uphill toward her house in snow so deep
the road is gone, the lover walks the tops
of fence posts. Thoughts about his dying child,
or how to keep the farm after the fire
never enter his mind. Not that he's so
preoccupied with balancing himself
in his work boots, but that the deaths of child
and farm haven't yet happened, couldn't happen
on such a luminous night, the gauzy moon
just rising over her father's roof as if
to guide him there. The only howling comes
from her dog, Shep, who has already heard
his lurching steps, and perhaps even smells
the hurt bird he holds in his coat, a gift
he can hardly wait to give. No need to hurry:
Soon, farm boy become impresario,
he'll lift his coat back from the kitchen table
and leave a creature there, dragging its wing.
Soon, cooing softly at its box, she'll shoo
her younger sisters out and shut the door
and draw him close, finding in his grave dark eyes
how well they've known each other all along.
Soon their long climb together will begin.

THE SECRET

How have we forgotten her,
the dreamy-faced girl
on this strange evening
at her grandparents' farm?
How have we forgotten
the mad aunt
who rejected her
for having such blue eyes?
Both are difficult to make out
at first, the aunt
standing in twilight
by the kitchen stove,
the niece watching how she stares
and turns to go upstairs
to her room, thinking then
she sees a woman
inside the old woman. And so,
the voices of younger sisters
and neighbor girls coming through
the window from the far
field, she rises
to follow the aunt,
and finding the tall closed
barrier between them contains
a small keyhole, kneels down
to look right through
searching she does not know
for what — a secret woman
combing out her hair?

The photograph of a man
placed on a throne
of bureau and doily?
In that door's eye she sees
old repetitious pears across a wall
and, reaching inside the small,
bare bureau to pull
a nightdress out,
her naked aunt,
now turning to show
in the very place where she
herself has just begun
to darken, a gray, matted
and forgotten V. This is the secret
the niece carries into the hall
with old furniture
losing itself in the dusk,
and into her own dim
room with its pattern
vanishing on the wall,
and deep into her brain
where she will never forget
the color that will one day
be her own color.
From some other world
her sisters call and call
her name, which she hardly knows,
lying there with both hands
between her legs, listening
to the shivering trees.

WHEN THE TREES
CAME FOR HER

If you've ever waited
on a late winter night
at the one stoplight
of a town like that,
noticing then the telephone
wires shining under streetlamps
like the dead wings
of dragonflies, you'll know
how stunned she might have been,
how she could have turned
onto the wrong route, the one
with the ice bone
down the center and no signs,
even for the sharp curve she barely
came out of. You've been on roads
like that in the pitch black:
a car far ahead
searching the tall trunks
of trees with its headlights,
unable to find out anything
more about the place you're in
than you, looking through your own
pinhole of light: here,
the blank-windowed ghost
of a shack, here the quick
constellation of license plates
on abandoned cars, there
where the car ahead once was, now only

more darkness. She might,
of course, have turned back, unspooled
the long, high wires she went on
winding toward her around corner
after corner. But by now,
beginning to feel how lost
she had always been, she was drawn
to the odd comfort of the scrub-
brush closing around her
on a slow curve, drawn
to what it might be like not
to return, which was when it happened
down the road, way down. You've seen
how trees can dislodge
that way, one by one, and drift
toward you until it seems they're all
that moves, while you just rest
there, floating in the light. The faster
she went, the more they came
to join her. Imagine
as she did, how they asked
her to relax, opening their wide
branches. Close by her window
a trailer passed looking in
with one lit eye. Somebody's hand —
was it a dark pine's hand? —
waved upside-down hello, goodbye.

COMING FOR BRAD NEWCOMB

The childish striped
jersey someone

has dressed him in,
his silly sneakers

upturned on the bed
do not, anyway,

matter: we've come
to see his old, dear

head blinking awake,
the pupils straying upward,

the great brow turning
toward us as if

listening. We've come
to lean close by

the bad haircut
he cannot see

to tell him
who we are —

and if this night his lips
become a thumb

and forefinger searching
for a page,

we'll ponder
the luck of all

his forgetting.
We've come to lift him down

and place him, chest
and knucklebones,

in his wheelchair, and take him
high above its spokes

carrying light
through the dim hall,

and when we pass
wheelchairs that bear

those others
like shopping carts

with lost groceries,
we'll wave a wide hello,

then wave goodbye
to the desk nurse, surprised

to see old Bradford, blind
and frail go by

imperial and smiling.
For we have come

to this closed, loveless,
spiritless place

to leave it, you opening up
the heavy door, and I

pushing him out
into the growing dark

not long, not far,
to where the grass

smells like Kentucky, where she
and he first met —

and if then he should call
as he has called

each night when nurses come
to silence him, the one name

he cannot forget,
we'll let Brad Newcomb be

there in the half-light,
the breeze

loosening his hair,
blind and awake

to the ubiquitous
speech of trees.

MOTHER'S PLACE

She doesn't think
about the lightning
that rewired her brain
and left

her arm and leg
powerless. She wants
us to see her new
teeth, tapping them again

and again with her finger,
see? She wants to sit
all day in the body
of the one we miss

drawling orders.
We're getting used
to her slow hunt
and peck bent

over the remote
while the TV jumps
channels. She's only trying
to find her stories,

we tell ourselves.
She can't feel
that her perm's lopsided
when she looks up

or that her chin's all
wrong. It's the false teeth
that make each
word she speaks

a mouthful
and each "s"
a small
whistle. "Is

that dogs
barking?" she wants to know
on her reluctant outing,
quad-cane walking under crows.

"No peace around this
place," she says dragging
the left leg
up. "No peace."

THE BIRD MAN

The white
of that stone cottage
still in my tired eye,
I bump my luggage
through the door and follow him
down into the quick gloom.
Silence claps my ears
as if I walked under
water, passing reefs
of empty birdseed
bags, toward the room
where the light comes from
and the woman sits, withered
under perfect curls,
offering me the rocker
beside her. Where does the son
who brought me here (Our
house is yours) disappear
to, I nearly ask, but she
cares only for this wild, cooing
dove, rounding each corner
of the room, then
landing on my head.
He likes you, she says,
in her small voice, and just
when I've had enough
of my taloned hat
and the other bird
whose wing is so thick

with growths it walks
in circles at my feet,
her eyes shine up at me
as if I wore an
aura, and she begins
to tell me how
she got unwound.
Not just because
of what they do to cows,
she says, holding them by the neck
in their dark
stalls, and not only what
they do to pigs, though cutting
their dear throats
while they skree
is bad enough. What they do
to the birds. And up goes
her finger to trace
the slow, electric
spiral that undid her body and left
it limp. Oh, there must
have been a thousand windowless
chickens crying
all at once in my mind
with their beaks
cut off, she says. And then
(the distressed bird rounding
the room again)
she takes her curls away
so I can see
her small, shaved

head: where they opened
the skull's bone
to stop her trembling. Here,
she says, and Here,
guiding my hand so
earnestly, so
eager to help me find
the pitiable, gray skin
that suddenly I am
holding the poor, cracked
egg of her head
in my arms
and singing a song
I do not know.
But my voice knows,
sending its strange notes up
above my flopped
luggage, above the sick bird
resting on the sad
suitcases of my shoes
until I, too,
am rising. Somewhere below
the mild-faced son
is coming back into the room
with his three bowls.
Below, the man who holds
the mother rocks and rocks. I
am the bird man.
My eye's
the white dove's eye,
its wings how I

unfold myself again
and again, trying
to make the small, stone
place that encloses them larger.
I sing and sing the bird's
lost, longing song.

THE LIFE

There is a moment
when the arms,
sent behind you

to locate the sleeves
of your coat, become lost
in the possibility

of the garment lifting
above them. This
is why they thrash

out of your sight,
searching not
for what you think

you want, but what
behind your own back
you yearn for,

a seamless place
that opens
to another life.

❧ HOUSE IN SPRING

Where it stands in the wind
unpinning the plastic
it has worn all winter

there is not one tree,
and nobody sees the long
remnants unfolding

in the late light.
Now it is tossing them
across the windowless

pair of shutters
and the great, swollen
place in the clapboards.

Now it is drawing them
back from the stairless
front door again

and again like an old
burlesque queen, alone
in the potato fields

of Mars Hill, Maine.

SEEING MERCER, MAINE

Beyond the meadow
on Route 2, the semis
go right on by,
hauling their long
echoes into the trees.
They want nothing to do
with this road buckling downhill
toward the Grange and Shaw
Library, Open 1–5 pm SAT,
and you may wonder
why I've brought you here,
too. It's not SAT,
and apart from summer, the big
event in town's the bog
water staggering down the falls.
Would it matter if I told you
people live here — the old
man from the coast who built
the lobster shack in a hayfield;
the couple with the sign
that says Cosmetics
and Landfill; the woman
so shy about her enlarged leg
she hangs her clothes
outdoors at night? Walk down this road
awhile. What you see here in daytime —
a kind of darkness that comes
from too much light —
you'll need to adjust

your eyes for. The outsized
hominess of that TV dish,
for instance, leaning
against its cupboard
of clapboard. The rightness
of the lobsterman's shack —
do you find it, tilted
there on the sidehill,
the whitecaps of daisies
just cresting beside it
in the light wind?

THE ONE WHO WILL
SAVE YOU

If some afternoon you
should pass by there,
and the woman comes out swooping
her blue bathrobe back
from her path and crying, "Baby, oh my
sweet baby," it won't be you
she means, nor you
the hubby wearing motorcycles
on his T-shirt and jumping
down from the stairless
sliding glass door
says he wants to kill, so just
stand still. It's the dog
they'll be after, the shadow
under the not-quite sunk pink
Chevy, ratcheting itself up
with a slow, almost inaudible
growl into the biggest, ugliest
shepherd-Labrador-husky
cross West Central Maine
has ever seen. It won't matter
if the two shirtless fat kids
come from around back with
hubcaps on their heads and shout
even louder than their father does,
"Queenie!" By then Queenie,
less a queen than a chain-
saw lunging at the potential

cordwood of your legs,
won't know or care what
humans have named her. There'll be
no hope for you, Pal, unless,
that is, the teenage daughter,
who comes across the front lawn's
dandelions in her tank top
every so often to set me free,
releases you, too — shaking her head
as if only you and she
could see how impossible
her stupid parents and this uncool
dog really are, and lifting it,
like that, by the collar
to create a bug-eyed
sausage that gasps
so loud her mother gasps — not
that the daughter will care. "Mother,"
she'll say, eyeing the sorry choice
of afternoon attire, "you should see
how you look." Then, flicking
Dad out of the way
and renaming the creature
she's created "Peckerwood,"
she'll march as if she
herself were now queen
back through that kingdom
of California raisins and tires
and Christmas lights decking the front
porch in July, and past the screen door
with the sign saying This

Is Not A Door, to disappear,
rump by rump with a bump
and a grind to you,
through the real screen door.

FRANCIS BOUND

All that spitting
and stuttering and rotating
his thumb-knuckle
fist as if to jump-start
his sentence. You almost
want to help him
though everyone in town says don't
get him started,
everyone except Dolly Lee.
He could be caught
in the waves of a "w"
all afternoon
and she'd go right on
smiling that tolerant smile
of a wife who's been living in her head
for years. She's the one back
in the shadows of the truck-
cab whenever he stops,
beaming. For Francis
will already be thumb-
knuckling and stuttering about what's
wrong and how it
got that way while maybe Ralph True
stands lifting and flopping
his baseball cap thinking god
damn to hell. Imagine any three
men re-flopping their caps
at the store window watching
old Francis drive in. Think of the women

at the Grange when he stands up,
reaching for their knitting. Think
of poor Francis, ransacking
the very air above his head
searching for the words
that say how bad it is
or how it could be if only
he could find them,
if he could say them,
if he could catch up at last
with the thought that is
already gone.

🌿 MAKING THINGS CLEAN

One would hardly recognize him like this,
the high-school shop teacher, glasses off,
bent over the kitchen sink. Nearby,
house dresses and underpants flutter
in the window of the Maytag he bought
for his mother. Its groaning is the only
sound while she washes his hair,
lifting the trembling water in her hands
as she has always done, working foam up
from his gray locks like the lightest
batter she ever made. Soon enough,
glasses back on, he will stand
before students who mock his dullness;
soon, putting up clothes, she'll feel
the ache of a body surrendering to age.
A little longer let him close his eyes
against soap by her apron, let her move
her fingers slowly, slowly in this way
the two of them have found to be together,
this transfiguring moment in the world's
old work of making things clean.

READING POEMS
AT THE GRANGE MEETING
IN WHAT MUST BE HEAVEN

How else to explain that odd,
perfect supper — the burnished
lasagna squares, thick
clusters of baked
beans, cole slaw pink

with beet juice? How else
to tell of fluorescent
lights touching their once-familiar
faces, of pipes branching over
their heads from the warm

furnace-tree, like no tree on earth —
or to define the not-quite
dizziness of going
up the enclosed, turning
stair afterward to find them

in the room of the low
ceiling, dressed as if for play?
Even Dolly Lee, talked into coming
to this town thirty
years ago from California,

wears a blue sash,
leaving each curse against winters
and the black fly far
behind. And beside her
Francis, who once did the talking,

cranking his right hand
even then, no doubt, to jump-
start his idea, here uses his hand
to raise a staff, stone silent,
a different man. For the Grange

meeting has begun, their fun
of marching serious-faced together
down the hall to gather
stout Bertha who bears the flag
carefully ahead of herself

like a full
dust-mop, then
marching back again,
the old floor making long
cracking sounds

under their feet like late
pond ice that will not break —
though now the whole group stands
upon it, hands
over their hearts. It does not matter

that the two retarded men, who in the other
world attempted haying for Mrs. Carter,
stand here beside her
pledging allegiance in words
they themselves have never heard.

It does not matter
that the Worthy Master,
the Worthy Overseer
and the Secretary sit back
down at desks

donated by School District
#54 as if all three were
in fifth grade: everyone here
seems younger — the shiny baldheaded
ones, the no longer old

ladies, whose spectacles
fill with light as they
look up, and big Lenny
too, the trucker, holding the spoons
he will play soon

and smiling at me as if
the accident that left
the long cheek scar and mashed
his ear never happened. For I
am rising

with my worn folder
beside the table of potholders,
necklaces made from old newspaper
strips and rugs braided
from rags. It does not matter

that in some narrower time
and place I did not want
to read to them on
Hobby Night. What matters is
that standing in — how else

to understand it — the heaven
of their wonderment,
I share the best
thing I can make — this stitching
together of memory

and heart-scrap, this wish
to hold together Francis,
Dolly Lee, the Grange Officers,
the retarded men and everybody
else here levitating

ten feet
above the dark
and cold and regardless
world below them and me
and poetry.

DRIVING TO DARK COUNTRY

Past where the last
gang of signs

comes out of the dark
to wave you back,

and past telephone
wires lengthening

with the light of someone
beyond the next hill

just returning,
a slow, single line

will take the eye
of your high beam. Around you

will be jewels
of the fox-watch.

Great trees will rise up
to see you passing by

all by yourself,
riding on light.

Part Two

MY BROTHER RUNNING

…

Out of leaves falling
Over leaves fallen
A runner comes running

Aware of no watcher
His loneness my loneness
His running my running.

Robert Francis,
"His Running, My Running"

I   It is impossible to stop my brother.
    In my fantasy, everyone tries. My mother comes
    from the nursery and truck garden
    she never wanted but inherited anyway after
    my stepfather's death. Look what happened
    to me, she says to him. Work, work,
    work, the whole place growing up
    into trees. For once in this family think
    what you're getting yourself into.

    My older brother Jim flies in from Alaska.
    Here I am, he says, shuffling
    around in mukluks with a truss on
    under my jeans and a shot liver
    from drinking too many 12-packs.
    So much for my big dream of finding the home
    where I belong on the frontier.
    Forget this running shit. It won't
    get you where you want to go, either.

    The truth is, nobody tries to stop him.
    My mother, fresh out of solutions,
    is raising chinchillas to save the farm
    and show the world how much she cared
    about her husband all along.
    Against doctor's orders, Jim
    is probably cracking beers for himself
    and this guy he has just met, a real
    find, one of the sharpest characters in Sitka.

I'm not even there, not yet, off in my own
world, no doubt, writing poems.
So there Bob is by himself
unaware I am now discovering him
at 5:00 a.m. in the dark kitchen
of his suburban house, 42 years old, 1985,
double-tying his Nikes. What amazes
me all over again is how fat
he has got, so bending over in his chair

in his sweatpants, he can hardly see what his
hands are doing, the fingertips
nail-bitten and bulbous, just as they were
when he was a kid. In his mind
this morning and every morning he rises
on almost no sleep, so high
it scares him, is the lovely
face of a woman, this one
he now takes out the front door

quietly, not to wake his wife
and children above his head, and there
beside his big American dealer car
and the trees untangling their leaves
from the dark, he begins to run,
fuck everybody, through the narrow street,
taking the air into his lungs as if
breathing for the first time, sending each
neat lawn, each white clapboard house behind him

and away until he is up to speed
at last with this relentless,
beautiful feeling, this terrifying
rush of joy whose name is her name
which he now murmurs, lifted into the high C
of his obsession, no mother, no brothers, no wife
and kids, no cars passing him, this oblivious man
with sweat opening at the center of his shirt, oh
my brother running too fast down the road to his death.

11   Don't think I don't notice it,
this thing that comes into my voice
when I talk about him,
but four years later, here's
how it is: I still find myself staring
at the puzzle of leaves outside my window,
suddenly awake in the dark just before
the time of his running and saying
No, right out loud, seeing only then

Bob has closed the door so lightly
and walked out past the add-ons
of family room and porch which never
made the small house large enough
in some other time; that my little brother
has already lain down in his bed
after six crazy months of it
and one last, long journey of his heart
while his wife climbed on top of him

and breathed into his mouth
and his little son, God help him, beat
and beat on his chest, discovering
perhaps the slightest smile on his lips
like the smile in my dream
when I tell Bob that someone has died,
someone we knew very well, seeing at last
that the one who has died
is my smiling brother himself —

leaving me with such
fragments! A red football
he threw twenty years ago
in the K-Mart, all the way
from Sports where he couldn't breathe
for laughing to Stationery where I
saw it wobbling down from the ceiling
and caught it right in front of the clerk:
telling him I'll never go into a store

with you again, and shouting
at him from my bed with the worst
hangover of my life, This is the last
time I ever go drinking
with you, while my crazy brother
followed my face under the covers, kissed it
with a cold beer, then lifted the bottle
high above his bobbing Adam's apple
and drained it. Loving my screams,

of course, wanting me to say I'll never
get into an automobile with you all those times
he pulled out in his big car to pass my poor,
anxious, dumb neighbor George Kohler
on a double yellow line at the same
curve, giving him the finger up through
the sun roof. That was the way
my brother was, doing seventy
and smiling that shit-eating smile,

knowing the next day I'd be right
there with him, just as he knew that afternoon
twenty years later when I opened the door
to discover him, grown skinny from all
the running — knew that when he smiled
this time, I'd be unable to say
I'll never go or get into it,
but would take the hand he held out and go along
and get more deeply than ever into it.

III   Still it was a strange moment to find my brother
suddenly there, jerking my hand — not the fat,
successful teacher and car salesman on Christmas cards
his wife had sent each year mechanically
and with much love, but this new
thin Bob with a rack of tall-boys
under his arm as if twenty years
had never happened. Except,
of course, this Bob had gray hair

and a way of going slightly
walleyed when he focused on you
so he seemed to be somewhere else
in his mind. Except he had his oldest
son with him, Patrick, the same kid
who in three months would be trying to call
Bob back from a heart attack
and who already felt something
was wrong for his father

to have driven all the way from Boston
to central Maine to see the brother
he almost never saw, the one his mother
never liked. So there, trying to talk
between the boy's quick, suspicious returns
from patting the dog outside, we were:
and there with that spacy
look in his eye, this brother
I hardly knew began to tell

his story of the small house
where the fat man with two jobs
and never enough money apologized over
and over to the wife, and the sad
acrobatics of their sex when even
her uterus resisted him, and the three
sons she had at last, whispering to them
and taking them to mass where she whispered
to her family, too Catholic after all

those years to take him in, and the whole
country-and-western breakdown of I can't
live this way, Bob spitting up blood
from the drink, Bob opening up
new rooms looking for space
in the house that grew smaller as he beat
and beat it with his hammer, nights, weekends,
year after year, walling himself into it all
over again. Until, he said, he found this

woman: and all at once, think fast,
her photograph came floating
down through the air from the same hand
that once threw the football, and he
was smiling in the old way. Except
as he bent now by my side
in the late lamplight, not quite believing
her picture himself, he was whispering still,
though by this time his son lay asleep

and my wife lay asleep, his breath
in my ear so in that family of whispers
I could hear the strain of the secret
that now bound me, the woman I'd never met
and my brother, high, exhausted, going out
to the car to bring in his strange manuscript
about our dead stepfather, and whispering,
3:00 in the morning, as if our day had just
begun: You're the writer. What do you think?

I V   So sometimes when I imagine my brother running
through the morning dark, he is thinking
about our stepfather — about all
of his fathers. Just leaving the shut lids
of clapboards behind him on his street,
just beginning to carry the woman's face far
from here, he sees the lit window
of his in-laws' bathroom drift by
above his head and they come into his mind:

she earplugged in the far room, dead
to the world, and he, the father Bob once
adopted, up alone waiting for himself to pee.
My brother wants to laugh at the poor, dopey dick
put to sleep by a million pious refusals,
then carried off to soft sheets
in the morgue of a separate room,
but instead he finds himself running faster
and weeping so, he cannot stop.

Or here is Bob tying his sneakers
in the dark of his house when the woman
will not come. He feels a slight
pain in his chest and wonders why
he is thinking about the father who left
one night for good, rising (as Bob himself
now rises) above the heads of his three sons
until he is a cigarette's high red star
until the star winks out

and my brother, turning toward the door
in his own dark, discovers
he is not only thinking of his father,
he is his father. And of course running
toward the woman, though she's
not on this street where fathers
and children sleep, nor on the next,
nor miles and miles away, where the great
carriers of cables rise over him one

by one like ghostly icons, impossible to reach.
Is it out here one morning, running past the strip's
dead end toward these, Bob sees the stepfather
rising over him on a bucket of mud
dug from the well? Above this father
of his manuscript, twisting high in the ropes,
the crossed beams of a tripod.
Beyond him, a truck backs, lifting him
as young Bob and I stand by the well tile

looking up. Now, half in French, he is cursing
our older brother Jim for jerking the truck.
Now he is breathing his asthmatic breath
and twisting toward Bob, who reaches terrified
across the well hole and cannot, does not dare
to grasp his hand. Or is the stepfather still higher,
on top of the newly raised house dangling
a hook? Does Bob look up to find him on the day
three skinny kids carry a rafter so big

they cannot lift it, so big my brother, running,
feels a weight now on his chest that grows
as he goes faster by this tower
and by the next, alone with his thought
of how roofless, how homeless he is
but for this huge rafter at his chest,
and how fatherless but for this man
in the clouds, shouting and dangling
a skyhook no one of them can reach.

V   When my stepfather died in the summer
of 1985, everybody in the whole country
seemed to be at the movies, watching the second term
of Ronald Reagan, who'd just come to town in a blur
of flags, won the nation's heart and was romancing her
in the longest feature he'd ever made. Big business
was up, defense spending was up, Christa McAuliffe
was in Washington promising to take the souls
of everyone who hadn't won the Teachernaut contest up

with her. That summer in New Hampshire, meanwhile,
my stepfather got down under the same junk car
he'd owned all his life, pulled out the transmission,
and in what must have been a mixture of surprise
and recognition, watched the thing roll off
its blocks on top of him and snuff
his asthmatic breath. It hits me now
that nobody was there, any more than we were there
when my brother, shortly afterward, sat in the darkness

with the woman in his head, bent over his Nikes.
The radio in the grass beside the collapsed car
whispered a golden oldie to itself.
In the barn behind it, broken hoes
and wrong-side-up spades stood there
looking at nothing, and far off where plants
broke out of their pots and vetch twined,
the rows of twenty-five years' worth
of a failed nursery went on falling

out of perspective, collecting the dark —
the whole weedy empire lost
to the Shop-Rite bush and tree concession
off I-89, and he himself now lost
with it: the father of his stepsons' trauma,
the father of Working To Earn the Joy
That Never Comes. No more anger
about the life which, hands full right
to the end, he could not grasp and take;

no more in those dead ears the voice
of his wife saying, you always, you never,
the voice become his own; only
the wild, repetitious stuttering of goats
unmilked and unfed in their pen
until I myself arrived to milk and feed them,
and my brother came, and the three of us,
all that could be salvaged from the dead
habit of family, went together into that dark,

my mother in the lead saying, What
is going to happen to me next,
Bob close behind with the flashlight asking
How could he have owned such a car, and I,
unable to take in how old my mother seemed,
how fat my brother had got and the death
all at the same time. Then my brother touched
the light on the old junker, deep in its tires.
Then he touched it on the matted grass

and while my mother, too bitter and tired almost
to care, told how Lloyd come over
to jack the damn thing up and pull the body out,
I saw the image of my stepfather's face,
free of its cap and floating in its hair,
eyes closed against the world of auto parts
and all the other pieces he could not
find a way to fit together, this world
which he now left to each of us.

VI   I see at least one
of the family dead every day.
Walking the dog, I end up in Chicago,
where I have never been, on March 26,
1973. Beside me in the front seat
of another car sits my abandoning father,
not in the least surprised I have joined him
in this moment before he goes into the supermarket
for more beer and keels over

with his own heart attack.
Holding the gearbox in his lap
and wearing no socks, he doesn't tell me
he knew Kennedy or just had dinner
with Kissinger. In fact, you can see
from the way his hands are shaking
he doesn't have a story left,
but this doesn't matter.
I've come to tell him it's OK

he ran away from me and all
the rest of his fucked-up life —
that running from me so long and so hard
is a kind of love. What happens instead,
of course, is he turns toward the door,
opens it with his trembling hands,
and leaves me sitting there with the hard
slam of metal on metal in my ears.
It is the same when I imagine

myself getting used to the darkness
underneath my stepfather's car. Lying there
closer to him than I have ever been,
I want to say it's not important
the two of us once touched only
with our fists. I want to tell him
I know how hard it is to get life right
the first time, no second chance. Neither of us speaks.
I make out the terrible concentration on his face.

Nothing I can say to my little brother
will make any difference either,
of course, as he stands there
beside the dropped car, banging
the flashlight slowly in his hand,
the conflict he feels just setting
him into motion. Two days later
he is looking down at the closed
coffin in such a composed,

proprietary way he himself
would never guess he is making
up his mind to run. Here,
if I could, is where I would
speak to him, here as he leans down
to listen to one more secret his wife
whispers into his ear: *Brother of mine,*
it is not you under that lid,
not you who will never get out

from under the ground, go slow now.
Still composed, my brother raises his head.
Nearby in the church, my exhausted, disoriented
mother is laughing among friends she knew long ago
as if after all those years of wandering
among shrubs and trees nobody wanted,
she is being given a party. All day
the poor farm women come with cakes
and casseroles to her door.

VII   All day while Bob's wife stares at their clothes
        and keeps her children together on the couch
        as far from harm as possible, the same
        newsclip of George Bush and Christa McAuliffe
        in the White House with big hands
        and flat heads plays on the shot TV.
        For my part, I'm gofering beer
        from Bob's 12-pack in the refrigerator
        while he travels from dead rototiller

        to failed water pump to tractor stopped
        cold in the tall grass, trying to make them go.
        You are not alone, I would say in the one
        more night coming down. *If there is a lid to lift,
        let us lift it together.* What I do
        at the time, though — not knowing anything
        more about engines than I ever have,
        and missing the drama of my poor
        brother underground trying to get out —

        is pass the tools and the beer and watch
        the whole evening unfold without a clue.
        Now Bob stands up beside the tractor
        in the growing dark, his hands
        hanging there as if stunned
        by all they can't do. Now he turns
        toward the barn and walks as if
        carrying the hands to where they can do something,
        anything, and I see then it is pure rage

that takes him across the field, all
by himself though I follow, afraid for him,
past the goats whickering in their pen,
to the death car where he stops and lifts
up the old hood folding it in half
like a bedsheet and pops off the air
filter and snaps the antenna and kicks
and kicks the front wheel until he falls backward
and I rush to help him calling Bobby, Bobby,

as I did when he pulled some crazy
stunt twenty years before. But my brother goes on
gathering the hubcap he sprang loose
and the other junk and heading for the house,
one hand free to open the door, which he does,
though I am right in his face
at this point asking him what the fuck
he is doing — pulls the gasping
door spring all the way back and dumps

the stuff on the floor. Looking around then
at those astonished faces, did I remember George Kohler,
or the clerk at the K-Mart watching the football
come out of the ceiling? Did I sense
Bob was somehow trying to free himself?
I only know that upset as I was, I almost
wanted to smile. There by my dumbfounded mother,
my French-Canadian step-aunt and uncle inched backward,
he swearing Jésus Christ, and she crossing herself.

Beside the couch, where Bob's wife crowded
the children even farther back in their seats,
stood skinny, pony-tailed Lloyd and his family
from the garage across the road, all about to drop
their plates full of the casserole they'd just
dug into. These were the ones my drunken
brother addressed, one foot on the air filter,
his voice filling my stepfather's house: Nobody's going
to put on my tombstone life's a bitch and then you die!

VIII   Ah, Bobby, when you looked at me as if
to invite me, then left the house to run
for the first time, I should have gone with you.
What did I think I was doing staying behind
to pick up that junk, there was so much junk
already, the stacks of newspapers, the lit, lifeless
aquarium with the diver on its side
under a broken pump, the blown-out TV flipping
Christa McAuliffe up out of sight over and over.

Meanwhile, you yourself are disappearing
beyond the arc of the night light at Lloyd's garage,
thudding down the road in these incredible
fucking workboots. If I had been here
with you as I am now, I could
at least have talked you out of these.
Hearing you strain for breath
already, this out of shape, all I can
think of, Bob, so help me, is your heart,

banging away at those arteries
that hardly open, and I want to scream
no again. I could have talked to you
about the stepfather you never did
escape from, or the wife you are beginning
to hate, or how your whole life suddenly
seems like one of the dead machines farther
and farther behind you in the dark. Except
that sometimes, Bob, when a car shines its

oncoming light on you moving your fists
back and forth above your stomach in this way
you learned as a kid in high school, your head
thrown all the way back, it is not rage
I see in your face, but a smile
that says you don't know whether you are
somebody's son or somebody's husband or even
in this world. In your mind, where the sun is out,
you are just meeting the woman, your secret

so perfect nobody knows it yet, not me,
not the woman, only you, gasping for air again
and again in your amazement. The wind in your mouth
is also in her hair, for after all that
lovely fumbling for the stick-shift alongside
your leg to get the brand-new convertible
out of the car lot and onto the thruway
for a test drive, she's got it up
to sixty and you are starting to feel the knot

in your groin which you call *lover's nuts,*
for Christ's sake, whispering it to me at 5:00
in the morning on your first visit to my house,
the worst case I ever had. In that spacy eye
you are a boy again, we both are boys
again discovering love, and you add, *I don't mean it*
in a dirty way, and then you tighten the laces
on your sneakers and rise with the same
crazy smile on your face to walk out the door

and run, as you do now in this darkness,
past the ghost farmhouses, past the well-lit
condos built to look like farmhouses
and into the dark again where each road sign
says nothing at all and a dim-windowed trailer
drifts far off in a field. That lost, Bob,
and the two of us also lost, you running
toward your death, I keeping you alive in my mind
though I can hardly bear the thought of your running.

IX   But how can I let go
      of the two of us? Where can I lose
      this memory of my brother? Just when I turn away
      from his running, I find Bobby sitting down
      on the floor of my apartment twenty years ago
      after the appendix operation that damn near killed him,
      making his absurd TV antenna. Somewhere out of view,
      his professors at the teachers college
      I attended and got him into are pissed off

      about the tests he's missed. Out of view, my wife
      and stepchildren and my desperate struggle trying
      to be a father and make a home. In this memory,
      just big enough for my brother and me,
      he is surrounded by shirts,
      and in his lap a Sears catalog is open
      to the antenna section and the particular model
      he is copying with coathangers. His
      looks like a deformed dragonfly

      missing one wing, which, carrying him another hanger
      in a shirt, and about as drunk
      as he is, I am only too happy
      to provide the wire for.
      What happens when my wife comes back
      with the kids to find us here, and how
      I deal with being so broke
      all I can afford for the TV are these
      drunken loops he now installs, or how,

for that matter, Bobby makes it
through his college term, the memory refuses
to say. Only that we are bringing more beers
and he is laughing his wonderful laugh
which says look how we screwed Sears,
because *Gunsmoke* is coming in. It was this same
conspiratorial joy four years ago
on my brother's second visit
to my house, another one of my brain's

favorite hits. I'm on a beer run
with Bobby, who's up from Boston in his great,
shining convertible that makes the trees shake
their red and yellow leaves down on us
as we pass like confetti. It's a beautiful day,
and on it he has come to tell me his new
secret: that he wants to get out of his marriage
to his wife, and his mother and father
and sister and brother-in-law, and the whole

death-dealing clan. I am so damned happy
he's driven all the way here to say this,
so glad I've got my brother back,
I feel like lifting the old
finger straight up just as Bobby used to, this time
to his hopeless other life. Which is when he jerks
my arm to tell me his other secret: the big
Detroit's-last-fling, smiling grille of a car
we're riding in is the one he sold — honest to Christ,

with no profit for me — to the woman. I just wanted you
to see it, he says, my gift to her, our home
away from home, then smiles his spacy smile
and passes two cars. Let someone else worry
what he will say if he's seen driving it, or that this
is the only automobile in the outsized fleet
he managed to sell all summer, or how he'll break
the news he's just told me to his wife. It's not
my job to worry. I'm riding with my brother.

X   But of course it was my job,
and for all I wouldn't
or didn't have time to see
about my brother traveling too fast
for both of us at the end of his life,
I can't help but feel it's still
my job. And so in the darkness
of 5:00 a.m. I sit up in bed,
thinking sometimes of my brother's hair,

of that alone. Bobby himself sits up
in his bed on his third and final visit,
propped on pillows in a small circle
of lamplight. He doesn't know I'm standing here
waiting for him to glance up
from his notebook so I can say good-night,
doesn't know I'm astonished
by how white his hair seems in the light,
suddenly understanding in this moment

that the twenty mistaken years he's been talking about
have really happened to him. That is why
when at last he looks up — my little brother
with an old man's hair and these
clunky spectacles — I feel the catch
in my throat. I'm writing, Bobby says,
smiling because he's so in love
with the woman and this new self
he's just beginning to know

and then he vanishes: and then I'm by myself
again with the things my brother wrote.
I don't get them out anymore,
having them by heart, the story
of my stepfather and all the other stories
he tried, top-speed, to tell, their scribbled
sentences throwing misdotted i's and the loose
banners of t's behind them on their way
after his relentless thought. On one nearly

illegible page Bobby is a child
struggling with his brothers to build
his stepfather's house. Yes, sir, Bobby says
as he's been taught to say, and lifts
his corner of the huge rafter and falls
and cannot lift it. His stepfather
stands in the sky above his head,
baiting him with a hook. On another page
the angry stepfather rises out of the earth

to dangle over a well. Recalling this day
did Bob think of how Jim, through with being cursed,
charged the truck at the tripod
and sent the stepfather unravelling down
into the mud dark? Did he remember the beating
that made Jim run to his other father
and go with him from bar to bar
while that sad man told tales of the sharpest
characters he ever met and didn't remember

the next day sober? Bobby's own story
includes only this father who twists
and calls to him over the well's depth,
holding out the hand he does not dare to take.
And now I turn in my mind's notebook to my brother's
strangest story, where he has placed himself deep
down in an open grave. Above him, the woman cries again
and again (in handwriting so taut and baggy at the same
time it's almost flying apart), What will I do?

XI On the day he died,
    after I woke to the ringing phone
    and asked the quavering voice
    too many times if it could really
    mean my brother, and after I drove
    my mother, my wife, and our two nearby sons
    in snow down into Boston, welcomed there
    by the towers that walked toward us one by one
    with spaces in their hands, and after we saw

    on the grainy color TV of the motel room
    where we dropped our bags the small, terrible
    point of light far off in the sky dissolving
    into smoke over and over, and the rerun
    of Ronald Reagan assuring all Americans the frontier
    still existed even though Christa McAuliffe
    and the other Challenger astronauts never got there,
    I saw the woman. Do I only imagine
    that her face, blank from her tears,

    resembled McAuliffe's face? All I know is
    when she came out of the crowd in the hallway
    at the funeral home and spoke my name, asking it
    in a voice that said at once who she was, I dropped
    my eyes as if I had not heard, suddenly unwilling
    to believe it was Bobby she and everyone else
    had gathered there for until I myself went to see
    the body in the casket, which turned out to be some guy
    in a suit under a crucifix folding his hands, not him

at all, but him, oh Christ, him.
And so at last I began my search
for the woman — looking for her in the hallway,
then in the church while the shut, shining
coffin was carried down the aisle by pallbearers
I did not know — feeling somehow if I could find her,
the priest whispering his prayer of death
would not be; nor the mother-in-law
with the rosary who hugged everyone,

in love with death; nor the businesslike
sister-in-law taking charge of death's last
details and arrangements; nor the tearful wife
relieved she had got Bob, who'd never joined
the church, a Catholic grave; nor even me myself,
seated with my solemn family and craning my neck
as the priest whispered, still unable to see
that my poor brother Bobby's final secret
had turned out to be the very life he could not

reach and take. For the woman did not appear,
and my brother could not, and the priest went on
talking about the Lord's obedient servant
Robert, husband and father, at peace in the house
not made with hands, and the two families drove
in snowfall afterward to receive guests in the house
with the add-ons which Bobby's own hands had made.
Snow rested on the hats of aged neighbors who came
to praise my brother for shoveling their driveways

on his last day; snow clung to the teachers' worn coats
and to the jackets of students who never stopped coming
until there was no food left for the brother-in-law
to fetch for his wife, and the spent, henpecked
father-in-law slept like the dead in his chair.
He was such a good boy, said the mother-in-law,
hugging my mother. I raised him to be, said my mother.
He taught me so much at the end, said the pleased wife
through her tears, he must have known he would die.

XII   Back in my brain, far back
before the three women share
their satisfactions about the dead man
in his house, there is another house
where three small boys are holding up their hands.
See? they say to the father, just back
from one more long trip. There are marks
from the mother's switch even between their fingers.
See? What does the father say? In another room

when my father has gone for good,
my mother's face is high up
in the sewing machine's light all day,
all night. Pins shine
in her mouth. I do not dare to ask her
why my father's gone. *I'll whale you,*
she seems to say. She is bringing the switch down
on my arms and on my brother's legs
like pins, like the whale's

too many teeth. *I'll be good,* Bobby says, *always
and always, I'll be good,* trapped in the jaws
of the whale, sick with his dread
of the whale. Forty years later,
on his last visit, my brother is still
waving his arms and screaming,
this time about his wife. Ah! Ah! Ah!
he says, this is what I do when I wake up
in the night after my bad dream of being trapped

to discover that the dream is my real life.
And I say you can't let her do this to you, you've got
to tell her, the secret is killing you. And he says
I'm teaching her how to do the insurances
and the taxes first, how can you expect her
to get by after I've left her, and I tell him Bobby,
Bobby where the fuck is being a good boy
going to get you, she'll hate you anyway
after the divorce. And my brother stops right there

on our walk together far off in the woods
and snow where a hundred leafless
branches are giving themselves to the wind
and the coming dark. You think I'm not going
to do it? he says lifting his bottle to drain
the last of his beer. You think I'm in love
with my life as a fucked-up entrepreneur selling cars
nobody wants, one of Reagan's boys? And up
goes the bottle through the trees,

a small football with no receiver save the wide,
luminous clearing ahead of us where it falls
disappearing under snowcrust. What I want for myself,
he says, staring after the bottle with his spacy
eye and starting to walk until I realize
he's not going to speak this time about his teaching
or the writing he's trying to do or even the woman,
but the clearing itself: What I really want
is to build a house a million miles from the suburbs

in a place like this — Jesus, will you look at it?
he says, and steps off the snowmobile trail, breaking
into a run. This is the moment — my brother running
and shouting on his way to a field
in the fading light — that I remember
when my mother says, Bob was so happy that last time
he drove down from Maine. And how, she adds, he loved
to visit me, in his old home. Outside the window
the road to Boston widens, and the great towers come.

XIII   I think of you, Bob, heading toward the field
        that vanishes as you run, and ending up in the house
        of newspapers and bags of chinchilla food and ghosts
        and secrets. Above your chair in a photograph,
        your stepfather stands wearing the uniform of a private
        in World War II. I cannot ask you to look up
        at the sadness of his assurance, just a kid
        on his way to teach three stepsons the Yes sir
        he has just learned himself. We cannot talk

        about the sadness in our family of motion
        without thought, or get to the bottom of all
        the secrets. I can only let you go on talking
        about nothing in particular and smiling, perhaps
        about the woman, or the crazy house you want to build,
        while your mother talks back and smiles back,
        and the son you brought again, Patrick, now just a week
        away from the day that will change his life, peers into
        the dark aquarium where the diver lies on his side.

        And in the winter darkness of the day itself,
        after you've left the bed you'll come back to tonight
        to sleep and die in, I can do nothing but watch
        you tie your sneakers. It is impossible to stop you,
        though on this morning, as on the others
        when you have taken the secret only I and the woman
        ever knew out past your dealer car and under the snow-
        laden trees, nobody tries. Upstairs your wife is dead
        to the world. Far off in New Hampshire,

your mother is awake, too, carrying a bag of food
to her chinchillas, obsessed with saving
her farm home. I see the poor old woman
picking her way with the same flashlight you held
in silence beside the fallen car. In another time zone
Jim is up, in the home he sought in Alaska.
I see him there, divorced, disabled, handing a beer
to some sharp character that his father,
whom he has never gotten over, would have loved.

Far away in Maine I see myself, bent over
a desk lamp among the ghosts of my own failures
as husband and stepfather, going into the world
of my poems. I haven't yet guessed how homeless
you are — how homeless we all are. And so we move,
as you now move, Bob, taking the air deep
into your lungs, running for us all. With this antenna
I've made out of my grief, bigger than the one
the two of us made long ago on a difficult night

and higher, I see you traveling past the snowbound
driveways of the old people you will shovel out
in your last eruption of energy as if trying
to release your own bound self. You are close
enough now I can hear your feet leaving the snow faster
and faster, close enough I can hear your heart,
how it opens and opens in spite of everything
it must carry as you pass your in-laws' blank
windows and your school, dark as a closed factory,

the woman in your mind, your breath hardening
to ice. It is so cold in Florida, the o-ring seals
on the Challenger's solid rocket boosters
are frozen. Nobody tries to stop the astronauts,
on their way past cameras impatient for their flight.
Far from home, McAuliffe continues toward the launch
tower, waving goodbye. And you, my brother,
though I have built the best house I can build for you
to stop at last and rest in, you go on running.

ACKNOWLEDGMENTS

THE TOWN OF NO

I am grateful to the John Simon Guggenheim Memorial Foundation for the fellowship which helped me to complete this book. I also wish to thank Donald Hall, whose criticism and encouragements have been indispensable to this book and to me as a poet. I am indebted to Robert Begiebing, Sacvan Bertcovitch, Thomas Biuso, James Cox, and Mike Pride for their generous support.

"The Hand" is for Malcolm

"Where Are the Quelches" is for Ruth

"The Longing for the Feet" is for Aaron and Bill

"When Paul Flew Away" is for Paul

MY BROTHER RUNNING

I am grateful to the National Endowment for the Arts for a Creative Writing Fellowship, to the Bellagio Center of the Rockefeller Foundation for a residency, and to the University of Maine at Farmington for semester leaves — all of which helped me to complete the poems of this book. As always, I am indebted to Diane McNair for her generous support, and to Donald Hall for his criticism and encouragement. Special thanks are due to Lucinda Hitchcock for her inspired and dedicated assistance. Thanks also to Kate Barnes, Robert Begiebing, Philip Booth, William Emerson, Maxine Kumin, Ann McArdle, David and Jean Scribner, and Charles Simic.

"When the Trees Came for Her" is for Charles Simic

"The Bird Man" is for Diane McNair

"House in Spring" is for Malcolm Cochran

"My Brother Running" is also for Thomas Biuso

ABOUT THE AUTHOR

The recipient of grants from the Rockefeller, Fulbright, and Guggenheim Foundations, Wesley McNair has held an NEH Fellowship in Literature and two NEA Fellowships for Creative Writers. He has won the Devins Award for poetry, the Eunice Tietjens Prize from *Poetry* magazine, the Theodore Roethke Prize from *Poetry Northwest,* and the first prize in poetry from *Yankee* magazine. He wrote the scripts for a series on Robert Frost that aired on PBS television and received a New England Emmy award. The author of four published volumes of poetry, he has recently completed a fifth collection, *Love Handles,* as well as a prose volume about poetry in New England called *Mapping the Heart.* He directs the creative writing program at the University of Maine at Farmington and lives with his wife, Diane, in Mercer, Maine.

THE TOWN OF NO & MY BROTHER RUNNING

was set in Bembo, a design based on the types used by Venetian scholar-publisher Aldus Manutius in the printing of De Aetna, written by Pietro Bembo and published in 1495 by Francesco Griffo who, at Aldus's request, later cut the first italic types. Originally designed by the English Monotype Company, Bembo is now widely available and highly regarded. It remains one of the most elegant, readable, and widely used of all book faces.